# TIME TRAVELING TO

# 1964

## CELEBRATING A SPECIAL YEAR

TIME TRAVELING TO 1964

Author
Robert E. Taylor

Design
Gonçalo Sousa

December 2023
ISBN: 9798870375199

# Surprise!

Dear reader, thank you so much for purchasing my book!

To make this book more (much more!) affordable, the images are all black & white, but I've created a special gift for you!

You can now have access, for FREE, to the PDF version of this book with the original images!

Keep in mind that some are originally black and white, but some are colored.

Go to page 101 and follow the instructions to download it.

I hope you enjoy it!

# Contents

Think it over, New York, Chicago, San Francisco.

# **Chapter I:** News & Current Events 1964

## **Leading Events**

### The Beatles Arrive in America, Fans Go Wild – February 7th

The Beatles as they arrive at JFK Airport for their first U.S. tour

The day the Beatles landed in America, they didn't just bring their gear; they brought a frenzy never seen before. Even officials at Kennedy Airport, used to dignitaries and stars, hadn't seen anything like it. "Never. Not even for kings and queens," one said. This wasn't just a band; this was Beatlemania, and it was about to take the U.S. by storm.

Originating in the UK, Beatlemania grew off the back of hits like "Please Please Me" and "She Loves You." But in the States, it was a whole new game. The fans, mostly young women, weren't just admirers; they were devotees. They didn't just scream; they shrieked. Their signs didn't just say "Welcome," they said, "We love you." This was more than fandom – it was fervor.

When the Beatles debuted on The Ed Sullivan Show, around 73 million people watched. Their concert at Shea Stadium wasn't just a concert; it was a record-breaker. But being this big had its downsides. John Lennon, caught in controversy, noted they were "more popular than Jesus," causing a backlash that signaled the beginning of the end of tour life for the band.

The Beatles on The Ed Sullivan Show

The Beatles stopped live concerts, retreated to the studio, and the world didn't just listen; it waited, watched, and wondered what was next.

Beatlemania might have started with "teenyboppers," but it ended up changing music and fan culture forever.

## Most Powerful Earthquake in U.S. History Hits Alaska – March 27th

On a day when the earth roared to life, Alaska endured the Great Alaskan Earthquake, a seismic monster at 9.2 magnitude – the strongest in North American history. For nearly five endless minutes, it shattered records and land alike.

The aftermath was stark: fissures gaped, buildings tumbled, and a barrage of tsunamis redrafted the contours of south-central Alaska. The waves, spurred by the quake, wrought havoc far beyond, with a colossal 220-foot wave in Shoup

Collapse of Fourth Avenue

Bay, and repercussions felt from Hawaii to Japan. The toll was heavy, not only in altered terrains, which saw Kodiak uplifted by 30 feet and parts of Anchorage sinking 8 feet, but also in human terms – 131 lives lost, 122 to the tsunamis alone. Chenega village was nearly wiped out by a 27-foot tidal wave, losing a third of its populace.

Ecological disruption, soil liquefaction, and massive landslides ensued. Valdez's port, a vital economic artery, was devastated, shaking the local economy to its core. Rated XI on the Mercalli scale, the earthquake caused damage worth $116 million then, around $0.79 billion today. Alaska's landscape and psyche were forever altered, instilling a legacy of vigilance against nature's untamed might.

Nelson Mandela at the time of his sentencing

## Nelson Mandela Sentenced to Life in Prison – June 12th

Nelson Mandela and seven peers faced life imprisonment after the Rivonia Trial, a pivotal moment in South Africa's history. Convicted of sabotage on June 11th, Mandela, Ahmed Kathrada, Walter Sisulu, Elias Motsoaledi, Andrew Mlangeni, Govan Mbeki, Raymond Mhlaba, and Denis Goldberg, were poised for a possible death sentence.

In court, Mandela's stirring speech epitomized his dedication to combating racial oppression. He envisioned a democratic society, stating his willingness to die for this ideal. This wasn't just a defense opening; it chronicled South Africa's racial strife and the African National Congress's turn to armed resistance.

While Mandela's comrades were sent to Robben Island, apartheid separated Goldberg to Pretoria Central Prison due to his race. Mandela, already jailed for other charges, endured a grueling imprisonment, facing sickness and solitude but never losing resolve.

Mandela's incarceration sparked worldwide condemnation, intensifying international anti-apartheid efforts. His release on February 11th, 1990, under growing pressures, paved the way for apartheid's fall.

Ascending from prisoner to South Africa's first black president, Mandela's life exemplifies the triumph of tenacity over grave injustice, his legacy a beacon in the global pursuit of freedom and equality.

## Pres. Lyndon B. Johnson Signs the Civil Rights Act – July 2nd

The Civil Rights Act, a pivotal piece of American legislation, catalyzed the battle against racial discrimination. Championed by President Lyndon B. Johnson, it outlawed bias in public spheres, enforced desegregation of schools and public venues, and made job discrimination unlawful.

Initiated by President John F. Kennedy in 1963 as a comprehensive civil rights bill, its momentum could have halted with his death. Yet, Johnson prioritized it, driving the bill through Congress with determination.

Lyndon B. Johnson signs the Civil Rights Act of 1964 in the presence of Dr. Martin Luther King Jr.

Despite facing staunch resistance from segregationist Southern Democrats, strategic bipartisan efforts led by figures like Senator Hubert Humphrey, Johnson, and Senate Minority Leader Everett Dirksen were pivotal in its passage.

A key part of the Act, Title VII, established the Equal Employment Opportunity Commission (EEOC) to enforce anti-discrimination laws. Though initially limited in scope, the EEOC's powers grew, reflecting a deepening commitment to civil rights.

With its enactment, the Civil Rights Act didn't just change laws - it attacked segregation in public businesses, revolutionized social norms, and laid a legal foundation for greater equality by addressing voting rights, education, and public accommodation, steering America toward a more equitable future.

The first Chinese nuclear test

### China Detonates Its First Nuclear Bomb – October 16th

Project 596, or "Miss Qiu," signified China's bold stride into the nuclear age with a uranium-235 implosion bomb tested at Lop Nur, a cornerstone of its "Two Bombs, One Satellite" policy. This momentous test paralleled historic detonations like America's "Fat Man" and the Soviet Union's RDS-1, announcing China's arrival as a technological and strategic heavyweight.

Mao Zedong, amidst global hostilities, deemed nuclear armament vital for defense and a lever to elevate China's international weight. His conviction stemmed from a legacy marred by invasions, underscoring an urgency to consolidate national security.

Despite initial Soviet aid, the West doubted China's nuclear autonomy, especially its procurement of weapons-grade uranium. The successful blast defied these assessments, necessitating a reevaluation of the global military balance and diplomatic engagements.

In Taiwan, the test stirred fears, fueling debates over strikes against the mainland and an autonomous nuclear initiative. However, American objections and logistical challenges promptly extinguished these considerations.

In the wake of Project 596, China proclaimed a no-first-use nuclear doctrine, articulating a policy of minimal deterrence. This declaration was a strategic move to discourage nuclear hostility and showcase China's commitment to a defense-oriented military philosophy.

## Other Major Events

### Surgeon General Warns: Smoking, a Health Hazard – January 11th

US Surgeon General Luther Terry with his report

The 1964 Surgeon General's report, orchestrated by Luther Terry, was a cornerstone in public health, firmly establishing the connection between smoking, lung cancer, and heart disease. Aggregating data from over 7,000 studies, it pinpointed smoking as a cause of lung and laryngeal cancers in men and likely in women, and as a factor in chronic bronchitis.

This report built on prior research like that of Doll and Auerbach, which had already influenced the U.S. Public Health Service to recognize smoking's dangers in 1957.

The report paralleled the UK's earlier findings and catalyzed health bodies, leading to President Kennedy's formation of an Advisory Committee. This committee's comprehensive review led to the seminal report.

The resulting Federal Cigarette Labeling and Advertising Act of 1965, mandating warning labels on cigarettes, was a direct response, marking a leap forward in health policy and the advent of heightened public health awareness.

**Sidney Poitier's Oscar Win: First for African Americans – April 13th**

Sidney Poitier

Sidney Poitier's historic Oscar win for "Lilies of the Field" as the first Black Best Actor at the 36th Academy Awards was a beacon of progress in the fight against Hollywood's racial barriers. Born in the U.S. and raised in the Bahamas, he confronted racial discrimination head-on when he returned to America. Post-World War II, Poitier immersed himself in the arts, advocating for better representation of African Americans in Hollywood, which initially limited his roles in major films.

His Oscar symbolized hope and the persistent struggle for equality, a struggle highlighted by the time it took for another Black actor to win the same award. Poitier's extensive list of honors, including a 2002 Honorary Academy Award, recognized his cinematic prowess and his dedication to racial equality.

Beyond acting, Poitier served as the Bahamas' ambassador to Japan and UNESCO, further showcasing his commitment to advocacy. His enduring legacy in cinema and activism paves the way for future generations, echoing his impact on diversity and equal opportunity.

**The World's Fair Held in New York City – April 22nd**

The Unisphere

The 1964-1965 New York World's Fair, set in Queens, New York City, was an exposition of American culture and technological optimism, despite lacking official BIE (Bureau International des Expositions) sanction. With the Unisphere as its symbol, the fair's theme, "Peace Through Understanding," aimed to unite the world during a time of significant progress. The fair displayed American industrial and corporate might and introduced the public to the burgeoning field of computers, operating over two six-month seasons. It attracted 51 million visitors, fewer than the 70 million expected, and charged entry fees equivalent to $9.44 to $23.22 today. Hosted in Flushing Meadows, familiar from "The Great Gatsby" and the 1939–1940 World's Fair, the event featured over 140 pavilions,

110 restaurants, with contributions from 80 nations, 24 states, and 45 corporations. Notable exhibits included Michelangelo's Pietà, a Belgian village replica, and diverse culinary delights. It also faced competition from Seattle and Montreal but managed to draw numerous smaller countries and private exhibitors.

Now, for many Baby Boomers, the fair remains a symbol of a hopeful era, a nostalgic snapshot of pre-1960s innocence, encapsulating the spirit and aspirations of its time.

### Ranger 7: First Close-up Images of the Moon – July 31st

The first image of the moon ever taken by U.S. spacecraft Ranger 7

Ranger 7 was a milestone in space exploration as the first U.S. probe to return high-resolution images of the lunar surface, making the Moon an attainable target. It was a crucial part of the Ranger program, designed to take pictures up to the moment of impact with the Moon. With six cameras – two wide-angle and four narrow-angle – Ranger 7 had redundant systems to ensure it could send quality images. In its final 17 minutes, it transmitted over 4,300 photos before crashing into Mare Cognitum.

This achievement followed earlier Ranger missions that failed, casting doubt on the Jet Propulsion Laboratory and the utility of lunar photos. Ranger 6, for instance, failed to return any images.

Yet, Ranger 7's success validated the pursuit of space exploration and demonstrated the importance of perseverance and technological progress. It reignited interest in lunar missions and laid the groundwork for future exploration. This triumph was a testament to human creativity and the expansiveness of our reach into space, firmly placing the Moon within our grasp and securing Ranger 7's place in space history.

Ranger 7 cameras system

## Che Guevara Speaks at the United Nations – December 11th

At the United Nations, Che Guevara, embodying the revolutionary zeal of Cuba, confronted global leaders with a blistering critique of imperialism and inequality. Leading the Cuban delegation, his speech dissected the UN's shortcomings in combating grave injustices like apartheid. Guevara's words, charged with the fervor of the Cold War's ideological battles, challenged the

Che Guevara at the U.N.

United States on civil rights failures and highlighted the interconnectedness of international struggles against oppression.

He eloquently recited the Second Declaration of Havana, framing Latin America's collective defiance against imperialist exploitation. Guevara's discourse at the UN extended beyond mere politics; it was an ideological call to arms for the disenfranchised globally, a voice for the "mistreated and scorned" against a backdrop of geopolitical strife.

This seminal UN address not only solidified Guevara's status as a revolutionary icon but also as a global statesman, whose revolutionary ideology resonated across continents among those in similar strife.

## Political Events

### Brazil Coup: President Goulart Deposed – March 31st

The Brazilian coup d'état drastically altered Brazil, ending the Fourth Republic and beginning a 21-year military dictatorship. Initiated on March 31st, the coup saw President João Goulart exiled by April 4th, replacing democracy with authoritarianism.

Goulart, known as "Jango," inherited the presidency after Jânio Quadros's 1961 resignation. His presidency, amidst social unrest and economic woes, polarized the nation. His progressive reforms couldn't stave off opposition from elites,

M41 tank and two jeeps of the Brazilian Army near the National Congress in Brasília

João Goulart

the middle class, the Catholic Church, and bureaucrats. Goulart's frayed relations with the United States, which opposed his leftist leanings, eroded his base.

The coup unfolded quickly, with military revolts in Minas Gerais. Goulart, opting to avoid civil conflict, didn't rally loyalist forces, leading to his swift downfall and exile to Uruguay.

The coup, initially supported by some hoping for a brief military stewardship, ushered in a repressive regime, aligning with U.S. Cold War policies. Historically, it epitomizes the era's political volatility and the trend of military coups across Latin America, fueled by global ideological battles.

**Gulf of Tonkin Incident Escalates Vietnam War – August 2nd**

The USS Maddox in the Gulf of Tonkin

The Gulf of Tonkin incident, which intensified the Vietnam War, involved a real clash and a misreported second encounter between US and North Vietnamese forces in August 1964. The USS Maddox, conducting DESOTO patrols, engaged with North Vietnamese boats on August 2nd, resulting in Vietnamese casualties and slight damage to the Maddox. The alleged second attack on August 4th was later deemed a fabrication, influenced by misread signals and doctored intelligence.

Despite doubts, President Johnson leveraged the claimed attack to secure support for increased military action. Skeptics like Pentagon official Daniel Ellsberg and Senator Wayne Morse challenged the administration's narrative. Morse, tipped off by an anonymous source, sought to scrutinize the Maddox's records to stall military escalation, but was rebuffed by Congress for his reliance on undisclosed informants.

Subsequent disclosures, including admissions from former Defense Secretary McNamara and declassified files, affirmed that the August 4th event was fictitious. Nevertheless, the incident had already propelled Congress to pass the Gulf of Tonkin Resolution, giving President Johnson extensive wartime authority to combat "communist aggression" in Southeast Asia. This led to full-scale US engagement in Vietnam, significantly altering the war's trajectory and US foreign policy.

**War on Poverty: Economic Opportunity Act Signed – August 20th**

President Johnson's poverty tour in 1964

The War on Poverty, under President Lyndon B. Johnson, marked a significant reform effort with the Economic Opportunity Act, targeting the nearly 19% national poverty rate. This act established the Office of Economic Opportunity to channel federal funds into local anti-poverty initiatives. As a cornerstone of Johnson's "Great Society" agenda, the act was reminiscent of Roosevelt's New Deal, enhancing the federal government's role in education and health care to curb poverty. Johnson's expansive plan launched forty programs to better the living conditions and economic chances for the poor.

President Johnson signs the Economic Opportunity Act

The initiative faced criticism for its ambitious goals. Conservatives questioned its long-term effectiveness and worried about creating a dependency on government support, while some liberals considered the actions too conservative. The enduring legacy of programs like Head Start and Job Corps highlights its lasting impact, though political shifts later reduced the focus on federal welfare programs.

Johnson's policies did see an initial reduction in poverty rates, yet the gains were constrained as resources were reallocated to the Vietnam War effort. Over time, poverty reduction has been uneven, sparking ongoing debate about the success and approach of the War on Poverty.

These discussions delve into the government's responsibility in welfare and economic regulation, reflecting broader ideological divides. Despite varying assessments, Johnson's War on Poverty remains a crucial point of reference in the narrative of American social policy.

**Malta Gains Independence from Britain – September 21st**

Gorg Borg Olivier after signing documents, granting Malta independence

Malta's strategic Mediterranean location has made it a desirable hub since ancient times. The Knights of St. John ruled for centuries until Napoleon took it in 1798, enacting progressive reforms that were at odds with the Maltese aristocracy and Church, sparking a revolt. The Maltese, resenting the French and their plundering, sought British assistance. In 1800, the British, wanting to curtail French influence and secure a naval vantage point, seized Malta and fortified it, turning it into a key naval base, notably for the Suez Canal route. During World War II, Malta withstood intense Axis bombings due to its strategic importance. For their bravery, the Maltese were awarded the George Cross and promised independence, which began with partial self-governance in 1947. Full sovereignty was achieved on September 21st, 1964, and in 1974 Malta became a republic. The final British troops left on March 31st, 1979, a day now celebrated as "Freedom Day."

## Other Notable Events

### Ruby Convicted for Oswald's Murder – March 14th

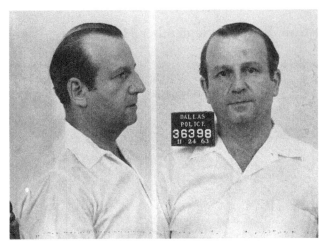

Jack Ruby, a nightclub owner linked to the mob, gained notoriety for killing Lee Harvey Oswald, the alleged assassin of President JFK, in a live broadcast on November 24th, 1963. Convicted of murder in 1964 and sentenced to death,

Jack Ruby's mugshot

Ruby's conviction was overturned over issues with his confession and trial publicity. The Warren Commission found he acted alone, driven by grief, but couldn't suppress conspiracy theories about his mafia ties and a mysterious "Davis" connected to anti-Castro activities.

Ruby claimed he killed Oswald impulsively while grieving, supported by his erratic behavior and possible drug use. His defense moved from a local lawyer to Melvin Belli, reflecting his unstable condition. His post-conviction actions, including tearful outbursts and urgent requests to testify to the Warren Commission, claiming a life-threatening conspiracy, only deepened the mystery. Ruby never got to Washington due to legal barriers and died in 1967 from a pulmonary embolism, leaving unanswered questions about his part in the Kennedy saga.

### Taylor-Burton: First 'I Do' Captivates Globe – March 15th

The romance between Elizabeth Taylor and Richard Burton erupted on the "Cleopatra" set in 1962, igniting a tumultuous affair. Both were married –

Taylor to Eddie Fisher and Burton to Sybil Williams – but their attraction was undeniable. Their liaison, fervently tracked by paparazzi, shocked the public and drew Vatican condemnation. Taylor and Burton married in 1964 after divorcing their respective spouses, and together adopted Taylor's fourth child, Maria. Nicknamed "Liz and Dick," the couple epitomized a glamorous, opulent lifestyle, spending lavishly on luxuries. Co-starring in 11 films, their real-life volatility echoed the drama of their on-screen personas, captivating global audiences. Yet behind the scenes,

Elizabeth Taylor and Richard Burton at their first wedding

their union was marred by infidelity, alcohol abuse, and intense disputes. Their first marriage ended in 1974, but the pair reunited and remarried in 1975 in Botswana, a union that lasted only nine months. This storied "marriage of the century" set a benchmark for celebrity romance. Overshadowing Taylor's later relationships, Burton remained her unparalleled love. Their saga became a benchmark for media attention to celebrities' personal lives.

## The Rolling Stones' First Concert Tour in the USA - June 5th

In the electrifying summer of '64, The Rolling Stones embarked on their first U.S. tour, igniting the flame of a legendary rock saga. Although not the vanguard of the British Invasion, their trailblazing journey would etch an indelible mark on American music. With their latest album in tow, they were greeted with a mix of fanatic cheers and curious jeers upon landing in New York – where cries of "Are you the Beatles?" echoed among the crowd of 500 fans.

The Rolling Stones rehearsing in 1964

Amid recording sessions and television debuts, including a less-than-ideal appearance on Dean Martin's show, The Stones faced the stark American reality against their British expectations. Tony Scaduto's "Mick Jagger: Everybody's Lucifer" captures the raw spirit and challenges of the Stones' early stateside adventures.

Their rise on the charts with "Not Fade Away" marked the beginning of a decades-spanning love affair with American audiences. This tour was more than just performances – it was the prologue to The Rolling Stones' enduring romance with the heart of rock 'n' roll.

## King's Nobel Feat: Youngest Peace Prize Winner – Oct 14th

Martin Luther King Jr.'s Nobel Peace Prize win at a young age marked a seminal point for civil rights, honoring his and countless others' pursuit of justice and equality through nonviolent protest. Despite enduring threats, imprisonment, and personal attacks, King's commitment to peaceful change remained steadfast, his recognition shining an international light on the struggle against racial segregation and injustice.

King, a Baptist minister and seasoned activist, was distinguished by his adherence to nonviolent resistance, drawing from his Christian beliefs and

Gandhi's principles. His powerful oratory, particularly during the March on Washington, left an indelible mark on history.

The Nobel Prize, while a significant honor, was a waypoint in King's arduous mission faced with FBI scrutiny and

Martin Luther King Jr. at the Nobel Prize Ceremony in Oslo

widespread opposition. His Nobel acceptance speech in Oslo resonated with his vision for a world where love triumphs over hate.

King's assassination cut his life short, yet his legacy endures, continuing to influence discussions on race and justice. His dream remains alive in those fighting against racial bias and for a truly equitable society.

The 1964 Summer Olympics Logo

**Tokyo Hosts the Summer Olympics – October 10th-24th**

The Summer Olympics in Tokyo, officially recognized as the Games of the XVIII Olympiad, were historic, marking the first time the Olympics were hosted in Asia. This event stood as a beacon of progress, symbolized by South Africa's exclusion over its apartheid regime, underpinning the Olympic commitment to unity and equality.

Technologically, the Tokyo Games were groundbreaking. They were the first

Olympics broadcast live across the globe, courtesy of the Syncom 3 and Relay 1 satellites. This leap in broadcasting allowed color transmissions of events, albeit partially, using advanced Japanese technology, which brought the Games into living rooms worldwide in an unprecedented way.

Yuko Shibayama wears traditional garb to watch the colorful opening ceremonies of the 18th Olympiad at the National Stadium

Scheduled in mid-October to avoid the city's extreme summer heat and typhoon season, Tokyo '64 established the importance of hosting the Games in favorable weather conditions, influencing the planning of future Olympics. These Games also marked the end of the use of cinder athletic tracks, making way for modern synthetic materials.

With 93 countries participating and 16 nations making their Olympic debut, the Tokyo Olympics were a testament to global sporting spirit. The United States led the gold medal count, while the Soviet Union amassed the most total medals. Athletes from East and West Germany competed jointly, signifying a rare moment of unity in the midst of the Cold War.

However, the Olympics also mirrored the era's political tensions, exemplified by Indonesia's exclusion due to the 1962 Asian Games controversy over Israeli and Taiwanese athletes. The Tokyo Olympics thus remain a significant event in the annals of sports and international diplomacy.

# Chapter II: Crime & Punishment 1964

## Major Crime Events

### Kitty Genovese: Murder Drives Bystander Theory - March 13th

The murder of Kitty Genovese outside her Queens apartment is a disturbing landmark in social psychology, infamous for the supposed non-intervention of 38 bystanders, as reported by The New York Times.

Kitty Genovese

This account, which later scrutiny found to be significantly misleading, fostered the "bystander effect" theory, positing that a person's likelihood of helping decreases when others are present. Despite the initial article's inaccuracies, which overlooked that some witnesses did try to help by calling the police, the narrative took a firm hold in the public consciousness.

The Genovese case is a complex lesson in media influence, illustrating how misreporting can shape societal beliefs. It continues to be a poignant subject in the study of social behavior and media ethics.

### Brutal Killings of Civil Rights Trio Uncovered - June 21st

The brutal fate of James Chaney, Andrew Goodman, and Michael Schwerner, young activists in the throes of the Civil Rights Movement, became a grim indicator of America's racial strife. In Mississippi, their mission to register African American voters met a violent end, culminating in their abduction and murder, with their bodies hidden in an earthen dam.

Their disappearance, initially a missing persons case, evolved into a revelation of deep-seated, institutionalized racism. The FBI's "Mississippi Burning" investigation unveiled a conspiracy involving the Ku Klux Klan and local law enforcement. However, subsequent trials resulted in minimal sentences, a stark display of the era's racial injustices, which nonetheless propelled the Civil Rights Act of 1964.

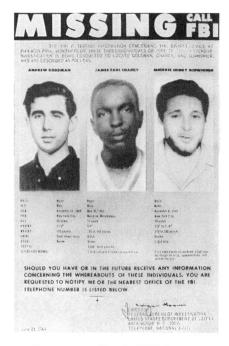

Poster created by the FBI showing Goodman, Chaney, and Schwerner

Years later, justice edged forward with Edgar Ray Killen's 2005 conviction, a delayed concession of the state's past failures. The case's eventual closure and Killen's death in custody are poignant reminders of the era's unresolved crimes.

## Last Judicial Hanging in the UK - August 13th

Gwynne Evans and Peter Allen

In a quiet, almost unnoticed manner, Gwynne Evans and Peter Allen entered history as the UK's last executed individuals in 1964. Their execution for the murder of John

West, just before the UK's shift away from capital punishment, went largely unremarked. Their deaths came just before the 1965 Murder Act, which paused and later ended capital punishment.

This underscored the contentious nature of the death penalty and presaged the UK's eventual permanent abolition due to concerns about judicial errors and the finality of death sentences.

Sixty year later, the UK's stand against the death penalty is a point of national pride and a beacon for global abolition, highlighting the complexity of the issue and the shift away from capital punishment worldwide.

## Brinks Hotel Bombing: Viet Cong Strikes in Saigon – December 24th

The aftermath of the bombing

The Viet Cong's bombing of the Brinks Hotel in Saigon, which targeted American officers, was a stark challenge to U.S. confidence in the security of South Vietnam's urban centers. This 1964 attack, leading to two deaths and around 60 injuries, rattled American officials who had perceived cities like Saigon to be safe havens compared to the countryside. It exposed the

Viet Cong's reach and aimed to erode faith in the U.S. military's protective capacity.

The bombing provoked critical reevaluation within the Johnson administration of the U.S. military's approach in Vietnam, exacerbating debates between those urging for intensified military action and those advocating a steadier course. Occurring amidst political unrest in South Vietnam, the attack also cast a shadow on the contentious leadership of President Nguyen Khanh, whose relationship with U.S. authorities was strained by anti-American sentiment and speculation about his possible involvement, despite the Viet Cong's admission of the bombing. This incident not only questioned the U.S.'s strategy but also highlighted the complex political dynamics at play in the conflict.

# Chapter III: Entertainment 1964

## Silver Screen

### Top Film of 1964: Mary Poppins

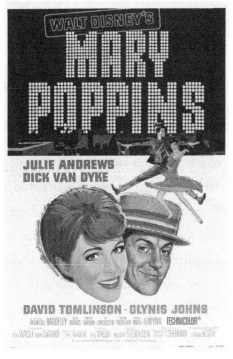
Mary Poppins

In 1964, magic literally blew into cinemas as Mary Poppins, with her iconic umbrella, and the jovial Bert, with his chimney sweep charm, graced screens. Directed by Robert Stevenson under the banner of Walt Disney, this gem masterfully married live-action and animation. Julie Andrews, in her mesmerizing debut, played the whimsical nanny, Mary, while Dick Van Dyke, with boundless energy and spirit, portrayed Bert. Together, they sprinkled enchantment across London, mending the rifts in a disordered family's fabric.

But the film's magic didn't stop at its narrative. Dominating the box office, Mary Poppins became 1964's top earner, amassing over $31 million in its debut. Garnering 13 Academy Award nominations, it clinched five, celebrating Andrews' radiant performance among others. With tunes by the Sherman Brothers like the memorable "Chim Chim Cher-ee", melodies from the movie resonated across continents.

However, its true legacy might be how it shaped the future. The unparalleled profits inspired Walt Disney to lay the cornerstone for what would become a monumental entertainment landmark: Walt Disney World in Florida. James Powers of The Hollywood Reporter lauded it as a "confluence of unparalleled talents," and it proudly boasts a resounding 96% on Rotten Tomatoes. Decades later, Mary Poppins and Bert's adventures continue to symbolize cinema's undying magic, melody, and wonder.

**Remaining Top 3**

My Fair Lady

**My Fair Lady**

In 1964, "My Fair Lady" dazzled the cinematic world. This musical comedy-drama, directed by the legendary George Cukor, brought to life George Bernard Shaw's 1913 play, "Pygmalion." Adapted from the Lerner and Loewe stage musical, it tells the tale of Eliza Doolittle, a Cockney flower-seller, and her audacious journey with phonetics professor Henry Higgins, played by the inimitable Rex Harrison. He vows to refine her accent, setting the stage for a captivating transformation in Edwardian London's elite circles.

Audrey Hepburn gracefully steps into Eliza's role, succeeding Julie Andrews from the stage. As Eliza navigates Higgins' intense teachings, audiences are treated to a range of emotions, from the celebratory "The Rain in Spain" to the touching "I've Grown Accustomed to Her Face."

Not just an artistic triumph, the film secured the spot as the second highest-grossing film of 1964, winning eight Academy Awards. Celebrated for its cultural, historical, and aesthetic brilliance, "My Fair Lady" has a commendable 95% on Rotten Tomatoes, solidifying its iconic status in film history.

JAMES BOND IS BACK IN ACTION!

EVERYTHING HE TOUCHES

TURNS TO EXCITEMENT!

ALBERT R. BROCCOLI and HARRY SALTZMAN present

SEAN CONNERY as AGENT 007 in IAN FLEMING'S

GOLDFINGER

GERT FROBE as GOLDFINGER HONOR BLACKMAN as PUSSY GALORE SHIRLEY EATON RICHARD MAIBAUM and PAUL DEHN HARRY SALTZMAN and ALBERT R. BROCCOLI GUY HAMILTON TECHNICOLOR UNITED ARTISTS

Goldfinger

## Goldfinger

"Goldfinger," released in 1964, is the third film in the James Bond series starring Sean Connery as the iconic MI6 agent. Directed by Guy Hamilton and based on Ian Fleming's 1959 novel, it co-stars Honor Blackman, Gert Fröbe, and Shirley Eaton. The narrative revolves around Bond disrupting gold magnate Goldfinger's plot to contaminate the US Bullion Depository at Fort Knox. Produced on a combined budget of its two predecessors, it was shot in the UK, Switzerland, and the US. The film solidified many hallmark elements of the Bond franchise, like sophisticated gadgets, pre-credit sequences, and humor. Notably, it won an Oscar for Best Sound Editing and grossed over $120 million globally. The promotional campaign included a renowned gold-painted Eaton image on Life magazine's cover. Lauded by critics, "Goldfinger" boasts a 99% Rotten Tomatoes rating. Premiered in London in September 1964, it faced a temporary ban in Israel due to Fröbe's Nazi ties, later lifted thanks to his protective actions during WWII.

Top 1964 Movies at The Domestic Box Office (the-numbers.com)

| Rank | Title | Release Date | 1964 Gross |
|---|---|---|---|
| 1 | Mary Poppins | Aug 26, 1964 | $102,272,145 |
| 2 | My Fair Lady | Oct 22, 1964 | $72,000,000 |
| 3 | Goldfinger | Dec 22, 1964 | $51,100,000 |
| 4 | The Carpetbaggers | Apr 9, 1964 | $28,409,547 |
| 5 | From Russia With Love | Apr 8, 1964 | $24,800,000 |
| 6 | Father Goose | Dec 10, 1964 | $12,500,000 |
| 7 | A Shot in the Dark | Jun 23, 1964 | $12,368,234 |
| 8 | What a Way to Go! | May 12, 1964 | $11,180,531 |
| 9 | The Unsinkable Molly Brown | Jul 11, 1964 | $11,070,559 |
| 10 | The Pink Panther | Mar 20, 1964 | $10,878,107 |

A Hard Day's Night

## Other Film Releases

The year 1964 was monumental in the film industry, introducing a plethora of movies that would go on to dominate the mainstream. Yet, away from the spotlight, six exceptional films made their mark, setting themselves apart and later earning the title of cult classics. These are "A Hard Day's Night", "The Umbrellas of Cherbourg", "Woman in the Dunes", "Kwaidan," "The Night of the Iguana" and "Onibaba." The Beatles were not just a musical sensation but also took the film world by storm with "A Hard Day's Night." Directed by Richard Lester, this mockumentary-style film offered a whimsical glimpse into the lives of the Fab Four during the height of Beatlemania. More than just a band film, it reflected the zeitgeist of the times with its innovative camera work and anarchic humor. Though primarily remembered for its iconic soundtrack, the film's ability to capture the youth culture and frenetic energy of the 1960s makes it an indispensable cult classic.

Jacques Demy's "The Umbrellas of Cherbourg" is a luminous musical where all the dialogues are sung. A story of love, separation, and melancholy, this film is adorned with Catherine Deneuve's ethereal beauty and Michel Legrand's haunting score. Despite being a deviation from traditional musicals, its emotive narrative and vibrant color palette have made it an enduring favorite among cinephiles.

The Umbrellas of Cherbourg                    Woman in the Dunes

Kwaidan

The Night of the Iguana

"Woman in the Dunes," directed by Hiroshi Teshigahara, presents an existential drama set in an ever-shifting sand dune. The story revolves around an entomologist trapped in a sand pit with a mysterious woman. A visceral

Onibaba

exploration of identity, survival, and human nature, its thought-provoking themes and striking visuals have cemented its reputation as a masterpiece of Japanese cinema.

"Kwaidan," another brilliant offering from Japan, directed by Masaki Kobayashi, is a visually stunning anthology of ghost stories. Infused with a dreamlike quality and punctuated by poignant tales of love, loss, and the supernatural, it has since been hailed as one of the greatest horror anthologies ever made.

John Huston's "The Night of the Iguana" is a torrid drama that delves deep into human desires, frailties, and redemption. Boasting a star-studded cast with the likes of Richard Burton and Ava Gardner, it's a tale of a deposed priest encountering various characters at a Mexican inn. Its rich characterization, atmospheric setting, and philosophical undertones have contributed to its revered status among classic film aficionados.

Lastly, "Onibaba," directed by Kaneto Shindo, is a chilling tale set during the turbulent times of 14th century Japan. A story of two women and a demonic mask, its intense themes of survival, sexuality, and betrayal, combined with stark black and white visuals, make it a hauntingly unforgettable cinematic experience.

In conclusion, while 1964 had its share of commercial triumphs, these six films, with their unparalleled artistry and distinct storytelling, carved a niche for themselves. Their lasting impact on cinema and the sheer reverence they command among aficionados make them the true, unsung heroes of 1964.

## The 21st Golden Globe Awards – Wednesday, March 11th, 1964

🏆 Winners

Best Performance in a Motion Picture – Drama – Actor:
Sidney Poitier (Lilies of the Field)

Best Performance in a Motion Picture – Drama - Actress:
Leslie Caron (The L-Shaped Room)

Best Performance in a Motion Picture
– Comedy or Musical – Actor:
Alberto Sordi (To Bed or Not to Bed)

Best Performance in a Motion Picture –
Comedy or Musical – Actress:
Shirley MacLaine (Irma la Douce)

Best Supporting Performance in a Motion
Picture – Actor:
John Huston (The Cardinal)

Best Supporting Performance in a Motion
Picture – Actress:
Margaret Rutherford (The V.I.P.s)

Best Director:
Elia Kazan (America America)

Best Motion Picture – Drama:
The Cardinal

Best Motion Picture - Comedy or Musical:
Tom Jones

## The 17th British Academy Film Awards – 1964

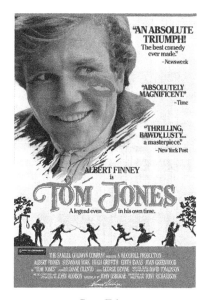

Best Film:
Tom Jones

Best Foreign Actor: Marcello Mastroianni
(Divorce, Italian Style)

Best British Actor:
Dirk Bogarde (The Servant)

Best British Actress:
Rachel Roberts (This Sporting Life)

Best Foreign Actress:
Patricia Neal (Hud)

Best British Screenplay:
John Osborne (Tom Jones)

Best Animated Film: Automania 2000 and The Critic

## The 36th Academy Awards – Monday, April 13th, 1964 – Santa Monica Civic Auditorium in Santa Monica, California

Best Actor in a Leading Role:
Sidney Poitier (Lilies of the Field)

Best Actress in a Leading Role:
Patricia Neal (Hud)

Best Supporting Actor:
Melvyn Douglas (Hud)

Best Supporting Actress:
Margaret Rutherford (The V.I.P.s)

Best Director:
Tony Richardson (Tom Jones)

Best Music (Song): Jimmy Van Heusen and
Sammy Cahn ("Call Me Irresponsible" from
Papa's Delicate Condition)

Best Cinematography (Black-and-White): James Wong Howe (Hud)

Best Cinematography (Color): Leon Shamroy (Cleopatra)

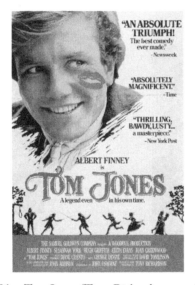

Best Film: Tom Jones (Tony Richardson, producer)

## Top of the Charts

The 1960s was a revolutionary decade for music, acting as a seismic shift from the traditional tunes of yesteryears to the dynamic anthems of a new age. The era was marked by the rise of the Beatles, embodying the invigorating spirit of rock 'n' roll. Folk music witnessed a renaissance with Bob Dylan's poetic lyricism, while the psychedelic sounds of Jimi Hendrix and the Doors expanded minds and playlists. Motown surged with artists like the Supremes and Marvin Gaye, melding soulful beats with poignant messages. Simultaneously, the spirit of Woodstock celebrated peace, love, and music. As the world underwent socio-political changes, the '60s soundtrack resonated with hope, rebellion, and transformation.

A Hard Day's Night

## Top Album: "A Hard Day's Night" by The Beatles

"A Hard Day's Night," released in July 1964, stands as a monumental piece in The Beatles' discography. Notably, it was their first album where all tracks were penned by Lennon and McCartney, a testament to their evolving songwriting prowess. The title track, heralded by its iconic opening chord, along with "Can't Buy Me Love," achieved transatlantic number-one status. The album's distinct sound, underscored by George Harrison's influential 12-string Rickenbacker electric guitar, paved the way for the folk rock/jangle pop movement. Bob Stanley, in his book, pointedly described the album as the epitome of The Beatles' early appeal, capturing their revolutionary impact on pop culture. Over the years, "A Hard Day's Night" has graced numerous 'best albums' lists, underscoring its enduring significance in rock history.

## Best Albums and Singles

In 1964, the musical spectrum vibrated with groundbreaking energy. The Beatles, taking the world by storm, released albums like "Meet The Beatles!" and "The Beatles' Second Album" while dominating the singles charts with hits like "I Want to Hold Your Hand" and "She Loves You."

Meet the Beatles!

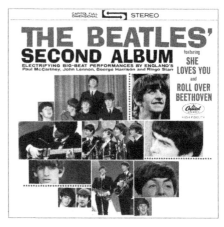

The Beatles' Second Album

I Want to Hold Your Hand

She Loves You

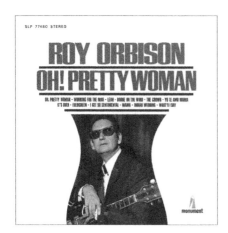

Oh, Pretty Woman

Roy Orbison captivated audiences with his classic "Oh, Pretty Woman," a song that became synonymous with his unique voice and style. Amidst these chart-toppers, the Righteous Brothers' soulful "You've Lost That Lovin' Feelin'" resonated deeply with audiences, adding to the year's rich musical tapestry. The sultry rhythms of Stan Getz & Joao

You've Lost That Lovin' Feelin'

Getz/Gilberto

A Love Supreme

Hello, Dolly!

Gilberto's "Getz/Gilberto" introduced bossa nova to a wider audience. John Coltrane's "A Love Supreme" elevated jazz with its profound spiritual journey. The airwaves weren't just about rock and jazz; Louis Armstrong's rendition of "Hello, Dolly!" seamlessly found its place both in the album and singles charts. The Rolling Stones and The Animals

The Rolling Stones

House of the Rising Sun                    Where Did Our Love Go

brought their own rebellious sound, while the Supremes' hits like "Where Did Our Love Go" heralded Motown's golden age. Indeed, 1964 was a year of musical innovation and diversity.

♫   Top Albums 1964 (tsort.info):

1.  The Beatles - A Hard Day's Night
2.  Stan Getz & Joao Gilberto – Getz/Gilberto
3.  The Beatles - Meet The Beatles!
4.  John Coltrane - A Love Supreme
5.  Original Cast - Hello, Dolly!
6.  The Rolling Stones - The Rolling Stones
7.  Louis Armstrong - Hello, Dolly!
8.  Henry Mancini - The Pink Panther
9.  The Beatles - The Beatles' Second Album
10. Bob Dylan - Another Side Of Bob Dylan

♫   Top Singles 1964 (tsort.info):

1.  The Beatles - I Want to Hold Your Hand
2.  Roy Orbison - Oh, Pretty Woman

3. The Beatles - She Loves You
4. The Animals - House of the Rising Sun
5. The Beatles - I Feel Fine
6. The Beatles - A Hard Day's Night
7. The Righteous Brothers - You've Lost That Lovin' Feelin'
8. The Beatles - Can't Buy Me Love
9. The Supremes - Where Did Our Love Go
10. Louis Armstrong – Hello, Dolly!

## The 6th Annual Grammy Awards – Tuesday, May 12th, 1964 – Chicago, Los Angeles and New York

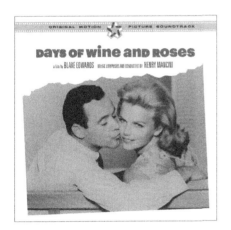

Record of the Year: Henry Mancini for "Days of Wine and Roses"

Album of the Year: "The Barbra Streisand Album" - Barbra Streisand

Best New Artist: Ward Swingle (The Swingle Singers)

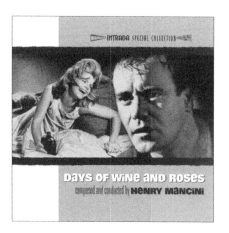

Song of the Year: "Days of Wine and Roses" - Henry Mancini &
Johnny Mercer (songwriters), performed by Henry Mancini

## Television

In 1964, television was in the throes of a golden era, carving a unique blend of innovation and nostalgia. America was spellbound by the bewitching charm of 'Bewitched', while across the pond, the UK introduced audiences to the rhythmic beats of 'Top of the Pops' and the enduring passion of 'Match of the Day'. Broadcasting had transcended mere entertainment; it was the pulse of a generation. The Beatles' iconic appearance on 'The Ed Sullivan Show' epitomized TV's transformative power. The television landscape of 1964 was a vivid tapestry reflecting societal shifts, unifying masses, and crafting enduring legacies.

### "Top of the Pops" Launches BBC Journey - January 1st

"Top of the Pops" revolutionized music television, offering weekly shows featuring live performances from contemporary artists and a rundown of the charts. Its debut featured Dusty Springfield and the Rolling Stones, marking the start of a cultural phenomenon that would run until 2006, securing its place as the world's longest-running weekly music show. Despite its conclusion, specials continued, celebrating major musical highlights. The show

Top of the Pops

was an influential cultural touchstone, highlighting iconic performances and trends, profoundly influencing generations of music enthusiasts and artists worldwide.

## "Jeopardy!" Begins Its Quiz Show Legacy - March 30th

"Jeopardy!" transformed the television quiz show format with its unique answer-and-question approach when it debuted in 1964. The brainchild of Merv Griffin, it challenged contestants to form questions in response to general knowledge clues. Though it saw several iterations, the 1984 syndicated version became the most enduring, with Alex Trebek at the helm until his 2021 passing. The show's legacy, marked by 39 Daytime Emmy Awards and global adaptations, continues in its 40th season, with Ken Jennings and Mayim Bialik as recent hosts, affirming its place in cultural history.

Jeopardy!

## "Another World" Brings New Drama to Daytime TV - May 4th

"Another World," an innovative American soap opera, commenced its notable journey on NBC in 1964. Created by visionaries Irna Phillips and William J. Bell, it unfolded in the fictional Bay City, breaking new ground by veering from traditional domestic narratives to explore intermingling worlds of diverse classes and ideologies. The show courageously tackled taboo topics like abortion, pioneered crossovers, and underwent various format changes. It also led the way with spin-offs and

Another World

charting theme songs, leaving an indelible mark even after its conclusion in 1999, succeeded by "Passions."

Bewitched

## "Bewitched" Charms Its Way onto ABC - September 17th

The fantasy sitcom "Bewitched" debuted on ABC, captivating audiences with the tale of a witch, Samantha Stephens, who marries a mortal and tries to live as a suburban housewife. Elizabeth Montgomery's charming portrayal, alongside actors Dick York and Agnes Moorehead, brought magic to viewers' screens. The show, with its unique premise and memorable characters, enjoyed high ratings and global syndication. Its cultural impact endured, evidenced by its ranking on "TV Guide's 50 Greatest TV Shows of All Time." The innovative blend of fantasy and comedy in "Bewitched" continues to enchant generations.

## "The Addams Family" Arrives with Macabre Humor - September 18th

"The Addams Family," a creation of cartoonist Charles Addams, brought their unique blend of macabre humor to television in 1964, after originating in single-panel comics. This peculiar family – Gomez, Morticia, their children, and an ensemble of eccentric relatives – thrived on the bizarre, often oblivious to others' discomfort. Their enduring appeal led to adaptations spanning films, a musical, and merchandise, culminating in the 2022 Netflix series "Wednesday." Their influence extends beyond entertainment, even inspiring aspects of goth subculture, proving the Addams Family's timeless resonance in popular culture.

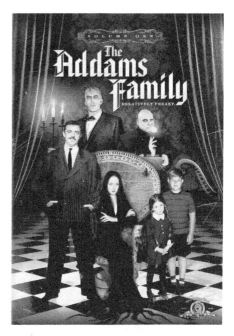

The Addams Family

## "Gilligan's Island" Sets Sail on Television - September 26th

"Gilligan's Island" sets sail on television, chronicling the comedic challenges of seven diverse castaways from the SS Minnow, abandoned together in the Pacific after what was meant to be a three-hour tour from Honolulu goes astray. The series, marked by

Gilligan's Island

their continuous, often Gilligan-sabotaged, rescue attempts, hinges on an enduring premise: people from contrasting walks of life, forced to coexist and collaborate for survival. Sherwood Schwartz, the show's creator, underscored this theme of necessary cooperation as still profoundly relevant today.

Rudolph the Red-Nosed Reindeer

### "Rudolph the Red-Nosed Reindeer" Makes Festive Debut - December 6th

"Rudolph the Red-Nosed Reindeer" Makes Festive Debut, celebrating the tale of a young reindeer who, once shunned for his glowing red nose, becomes the hero that guides Santa's sleigh through inclement weather on Christmas Eve. Rudolph, a creation of Robert L. May, first captured hearts in a 1939 booklet published by Montgomery Ward. His journey from outcast to beacon of hope mirrors the quintessential American Dream, spotlighting the unique gifts within each individual. This enduring character has found new life across various media, including the famed song, multiple movies, and a beloved television special by Rankin/Bass. His iconic status was further cemented with a series of commemorative stamps issued by the United States Postal Service.

 Television Ratings 1964 (classic-tv.com)

### 1963-64 Shows

| Rank | Show | Estimated Audience |
| --- | --- | --- |
| 1 | The Beverly Hillbillies | 20,175,600 |
| 2 | Bonanza | 19,040,400 |

| 3 | The Dick Van Dyke Show | 17,182,800 |
| 4 | Petticoat Junction | 15,634,800 |
| 5 | The Andy Griffith Show | 15,170,400 |
| 6 | The Lucy Show | 14,499,600 |
| 7 | Candid Camera | 14,293,200 |
| 8 | The Ed Sullivan Show | 14,190,000 |
| 9 | The Danny Thomas Show | 13,777,200 |
| 10 | My Favorite Martian | 13,570,800 |

## 1964-65 Shows

| Rank | Show | Estimated Audience |
| --- | --- | --- |
| 1 | Bonanza | 19,130,100 |
| 2 | Bewitched | 16,337,000 |
| 3 | Gomer Pyle, U.S.M.C. | 16,178,900 |
| 4 | The Andy Griffith Show | 14,914,100 |
| 5 | The Fugitive | 14,703,300 |
| 6 | The Red Skelton Show | 14,439,800 |
| 7 | The Dick Van Dyke Show | 14,281,700 |
| 8 | The Lucy Show | 14,018,200 |
| 9 | Peyton Place II | 13,912,800 |
| 10 | Combat | 13,754,700 |

## The 21st Golden Globe Awards – Wednesday, March 11th, 1964

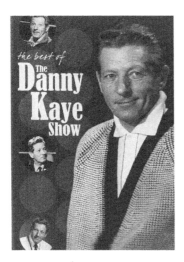

Best Variety Series:
The Danny Kaye Show

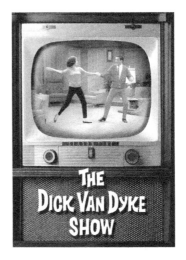

Best Comedy Series:
The Dick Van Dyke Show

Best Drama Series:
The Richard Boone Show

Best TV Star - Male:
Mickey Rooney (Mickey)

Best TV Star - Female:
Inger Stevens (The Farmer's
Daughter)

# Chapter IV: Sports Review 1964

## American Sports

### Richard Petty Wins Daytona 500 – February 23rd

Richard Petty in front of his #43 Dodge Plymouth

At the revered Daytona International Speedway in Daytona Beach, Florida, the Daytona 500 saw racing legend Richard Petty dominate the track. Driving a 1964 Plymouth, Petty showcased unparalleled skill, leading a remarkable 184 out of 200 laps, a record that remains unbroken. His win was pivotal for the Chrysler teams, who made a striking impression by securing four of the top five positions, especially with the debut of their powerful 426 ci Chrysler Hemi engine. This iconic race also marked significant firsts and lasts for many drivers, including notable appearances by Bobby Isaac, Dave MacDonald, and the legendary Fireball Roberts. Elevating the stakes, this event was NASCAR's first race to boast a purse exceeding $100,000, underlining its monumental status in the racing world.

### Boston Celtics Capture NBA Championship – April 26th

In the riveting 1964 NBA playoffs, the Boston Celtics, led by coach Red Auerbach, showcased their dominance by clinching their 6th consecutive

San Francisco Warriors playoff game vs the Boston Celtics

NBA title. Facing off against the San Francisco Warriors and the towering prowess of Wilt Chamberlain, the Celtics triumphed in a best-of-seven series with a 4–1 victory. With legendary players like Bill Russell and John Havlicek on their roster, the Celtics solidified their place in basketball history. This championship marked the inaugural NBA Finals face-off between basketball giants Russell and Chamberlain, with both leaving an indelible mark on the court. Their intense rivalry and the consistent excellence of both teams would continue to shape the narrative of the NBA for years to come.

### Ken Venturi Claims US Open Victory – June 20th

In the scorching heat of the 64th U.S. Open at Maryland's Congressional Country Club, Ken Venturi defied medical advice to retire, combating

Ken Venturi making the final putt on the 18th green

severe dehydration with tea and salt tablets. He persevered through the oppressive conditions, overtaking Tommy Jacobs – who had started strong with a round of 64 – to triumph by four strokes, setting new U.S. Open records for both 54 and 36-hole scores. Venturi's extraordinary resolve under adverse conditions and his historic victory were underscored as he played alongside the future champion Raymond Floyd, adding to the tournament's dramatic shift in narrative.

### Maria Bueno Seizes US Open Women's Singles Title – September 12th

Maria Bueno holds the Wimbledon trophy

Maria Bueno, the top-seeded player, displayed her tennis prowess at the 1964 U.S. National Championships by securing the women's singles title. Demonstrating her formidable skills, she overpowered Carole Graebner in the final with a resounding 6–1, 6–0 victory. Bueno's path to the championship wasn't without its challenges. She faced strong competition from other seeded players, including the likes of Billie Jean Moffitt, Lesley Turner, and Nancy Richey. In the semifinals, Bueno ousted Carol Hanks with a score of 6–4, 6–2, setting up her dominating performance against Graebner in the final. This win further solidified Bueno's place as a leading figure in the world of women's tennis during her era.

## British Sports

### England, Scotland, and Ireland Share British Home Championship – April 15th

The 1963–64 British Home Championship culminated in a shared victory among the England, Scotland, and Ireland football teams. All teams achieved four points by defeating Wales and having mixed results in their other games. Had goal difference been considered, England would've ranked first with a +8 difference, followed by Scotland and then Ireland. England started strong with a 4-0 win over Wales, while Ireland narrowly beat Scotland. A highlight was England's 8-3 victory against Ireland, featuring hat-tricks by Jimmy Greaves and Terry Paine.

Northern Ireland legend George Best (right) tackles England's World Cup winner George Cohen

Scotland's John White, who scored against Wales, tragically passed away two months post-tournament. In the end, Ireland bested Wales, and Scotland narrowly defeated England 1-0, resulting in the three-way title share.

## West Ham United Claims First FA Cup – May 2nd

West Ham United celebrates its victory

The 83rd FA Cup final saw West Ham United triumph over Preston North End at Wembley Stadium, marking West Ham's inaugural FA Cup win. Captained by Bobby Moore and under manager Ron Greenwood, West Ham managed a 3–2 victory.

Although Second Division Preston secured the lead twice with goals from Doug Holden and Alex Dawson, West Ham responded with equalizers from John Sissons and Geoff Hurst. The pivotal moment came when Ronnie Boyce netted the winning goal for West Ham in the game's dying moments. Notably, Preston's Howard Kendall played as the then-youngest participant in a Wembley FA Cup Final at 17 years and 345 days, a record later surpassed by Paul Allen in 1980.

**Fred Trueman Achieves 300 Test Cricket Wickets First – August 15th**

Fred Trueman, renowned as "Fiery Fred", etched his name in cricket's history by becoming the first bowler to claim 300 wickets in Test matches. The English cricketer played for both Yorkshire County Cricket Club and the national team. Apart from his bowling prowess, Trueman was a commendable fielder and a handy late-order batsman. He earned his Yorkshire cap in 1951 and was named the "Young Cricketer of the Year" in 1952. Despite occasional conflicts with the cricket establishment, Trueman's legacy in the sport remains

Fred Trueman in action

unmatched, leading to accolades like being dubbed the "greatest living Yorkshireman" by British PM Harold Wilson.

**Mary Rand Leaps to Historic Olympic Gold for Britain – October 14th**

In the Summer Olympics held in Tokyo, British track and field athlete Mary Rand made history by winning gold in the long jump and breaking the world record with a leap of 6.76m. This remarkable achievement marked her as the first British female to win an Olympic gold in track and field. During the event, she initially set a British record with a jump of 6.59m. Notably, Rand's Tokyo Olympics journey didn't end with this triumph; she achieved a silver in the pentathlon and a bronze in the 4×100 metres relay. Her astonishing talent was evident, with fellow athlete Ann Packer describing her as "the most gifted athlete" she had ever witnessed.

Mary Rand

## International Sports

### Heavyweight Upset: Clay Defeats Liston in Shocking Win – February 25th

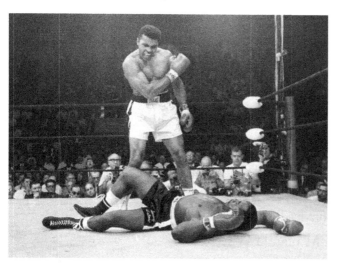

Sonny Liston loses his heavyweight title to Cassius Clay

In a staggering turn of events in Miami Beach, Florida, Cassius Clay (later known as Muhammad Ali) defeated the seemingly invincible Sonny Liston for the World Heavyweight Championship. Entering the bout as a significant 8–1 underdog, Clay's victory stunned the boxing world when Liston, the reigning champion, surrendered at the opening of the seventh round. Prior to this upset, Liston had been deemed one of the best heavyweight boxers ever, having dominated top contenders and previously knocking out Floyd Patterson twice in the first round. Liston's intimidating presence had even led British champion, Henry Cooper, to state he'd only face the winner if Clay prevailed. This historic bout marked the rise of Ali and left an indelible mark on boxing history.

### Dawn Fraser's Historic Tokyo Hat-Trick: Third 100m Gold – October 14th

Dawn Fraser makes Olympic history

At the Tokyo Olympics, Australian swimmer Dawn Fraser became the first to win three consecutive golds in the 100-meter freestyle, a historic swimming hat-trick. Renowned as an all-time great, Fraser was one of only four to win the same individual Olympic event thrice. Her dominance in the event lasted 15 years, and in 1962, she broke ground as the first woman to swim the 100 meters freestyle in under a minute – a record that stood until eight years post her retirement. Her Olympic triumphs were shadowed by personal loss, as she mourned her mother's death in a car crash shortly before the 1964 Games.

### Abebe Bikila: First to Achieve Two Olympic Marathon Triumphs – October 21st

Abebe Bikila, an Ethiopian marathoner, is celebrated for winning consecutive Olympic marathons, a first in history. His victories at the 1960 Rome Olympics – where he ran barefoot – and the 1964 Tokyo Olympics were both in world record times. Bikila not only triumphed in athletics but also sparked East Africa's long-distance running success, influencing

Abebe Bikila

future stars like Mamo Wolde and Haile Gebrselassie. After a severe car accident in 1969 resulted in paralysis, Bikila's resilient spirit led him to compete in archery and table tennis at precursor events to the Paralympic Games. His death at 41 did little to dim his legacy, which endures in places such as Addis Ababa's Abebe Bikila Stadium.

## Latynina Secures Her Place in Olympic History at Tokyo – October 24th

Soviet gymnast Larisa Latynina set a lofty benchmark in Olympic history with her haul of 18 medals from 1956 to 1964, a record unbroken for nearly half a century. Starting her Olympic conquest in Melbourne in 1956,

Larisa Latynina at the Olympic Games in Tokyo

Latynina clinched the all-around and led her team to gold. By the 1960 Rome Games, her preeminence was undisputed as she defended her all-around and floor exercise titles, among other wins. In Tokyo 1964, despite the rise of competitor Věra Čáslavská, she secured an impressive two golds, a silver, and two bronzes. With nine golds in total, Latynina not only shone in almost every event she competed in but also indelibly influenced gymnastics, highlighting her unparalleled skill and legacy in the sport.

# Chapter V: General 1964

## Pop Culture

Playbill Cover: Hello, Dolly!

### "Hello, Dolly!" Opens on Broadway – January 16th

"Hello, Dolly!", a musical masterpiece by Jerry Herman and Michael Stewart, opened on Broadway in 1964. Originating from Thornton Wilder's 1938 play "The Merchant of Yonkers", it revolves around Dolly Gallagher Levi, a tenacious matchmaker in Yonkers, New York. With its debut at Detroit's Fisher Theater in 1963, the show transitioned to Broadway, securing 10 Tony Awards, including Best Musical – a record it held for nearly four decades. The iconic soundtrack was later immortalized in the Grammy Hall of Fame in 2002. Its influence extended to cinema, with the 1969 film adaptation winning three Academy Awards. Over the years, its legacy has thrived through numerous revivals and international acclaim.

### Bob Dylan Releases "The Times They Are a-Changin'" – February 10th

Bob Dylan's pivotal album, "The Times They Are a-Changin'", marked a significant departure for the trailblazing artist. Shunning covers, this was Dylan's first album featuring solely his own compositions. Through raw and poignant ballads, he bravely tackled the era's hottest topics: from racism to sweeping social change. The title track, resonating with the spirit of the 1960s, became emblematic of an age of upheaval. While some critics yearned for the playful versatility of his earlier work, the album achieved No. 20 in the US and a belated No. 4 in the UK, cementing its iconic status in music history.

The Times They Are a-Changin'

## First Buffalo Wings Served at Anchor Bar - March 4th

Anchor Bar in 1964

On a chilly night in 1964, Anchor Bar's Teressa Bellissimo transformed the culinary scene by introducing the world to Buffalo wings. Meant as a quick fix for hungry patrons, this ingenious creation – deep-fried chicken wings coated in a tangy cayenne-vinegar sauce – ignited a nationwide sensation. Now a beloved staple, over 27 billion wings are savored yearly in the U.S. alone. Served with celery and blue cheese, Buffalo wings have become an American icon, their influence extending beyond the bar to flavor countless dishes across the culinary spectrum.

The Rolling Stones album

## The Rolling Stones Debut Album Hits the Scene – April 16th

"The Rolling Stones," the debut album from the iconic English band, hit shelves courtesy of Decca Records. While the UK enjoyed the album's raw energy first, the US audience anticipated its release under the title "England's Newest Hit Makers." Primarily rooted in R&B, the album showcases the band's profound love for the genre. Notably, Mick Jagger and Keith Richards presented "Tell Me (You're Coming Back)," marking their early songwriting efforts. Lending their touch to the recording sessions were Phil Spector and Gene Pitney, affectionately acknowledged in "Now I've Got a Witness."

## Mary Quant's Miniskirt Revolutionizes Fashion – Throughout 1964

Mary Quant, a British fashion icon, revolutionized 1960s fashion with her introduction of the miniskirt. Although the miniskirt's origin remains debated – with some crediting designers like John Bates or André Courrèges – Quant's influence is undeniable. She envisioned a skirt allowing women freedom and movement. Inspired by the energetic vibe of King's Road, she named her design after her favorite car, the Mini. The miniskirt epitomized an assertive

Quant wearing a miniskirt with flat boots

femininity and was popularized globally by the iconic model, Twiggy. Beyond the miniskirt, Quant's trendsetting extended to vibrant, patterned tights, leaving an indelible mark on fashion history.

### Barbra Streisand's "People" Album Hits No. 1 – October 31st

Barbra Streisand's "People" Album

Barbra Streisand's fourth album, "People," featuring the hit from "Funny Girl," topped the Billboard charts and stayed there for five weeks, earning Platinum status. Celebrated with a special plaque and immortalized by its iconic cover by Don Bronstein, the album's significance was acknowledged with its addition to the National Recording Registry in 2017. Streisand's blend of vocal talent and artistic expression on the album also earned her multiple Grammy awards.

 **Most Popular Books from 1964 (goodreads.com)**

- ✶ Charlie and the Chocolate Factory (Charlie Bucket, #1) - Roald Dahl

- ✶ The Giving Tree - Shel Silverstein

- ✶ Harriet the Spy - Louise Fitzhugh

- ✶ Nerve - Dick Francis

- ✶ A Moveable Feast - Ernest Hemingway

- ✶ A Caribbean Mystery (Miss Marple, #10) - Agatha Christie

- ✶ The Secret Life of Walter Mitty and Other Pieces - James Thurber

* The Book of Three (The Chronicles of Prydain, #1) - Lloyd Alexander

* Bread and Jam for Frances - Russell Hoban

* Why We Can't Wait - Martin Luther King Jr.

* Chitty Chitty Bang Bang (Chitty Chitty Bang Bang, #1) - Ian Fleming

* I Never Promised You a Rose Garden - Hannah Green

* A Nation of Immigrants - John F. Kennedy

* A Day in the Life of President Kennedy - Jim Bishop

## Technological Advancements

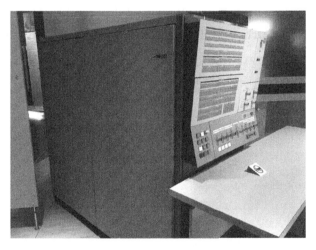

IBM System/360 Model 30 central processor unit (CPU)

**IBM Unveils System/360: A Computing Milestone - April 7th**

IBM's System/360, a versatile mainframe for everything from small business to advanced scientific tasks, changed computing with its unique architecture that separated function from design, enabling scalable solutions. Its Solid Logic Technology meant efficiency in a smaller package. The 1967 Model 91 exemplified its capabilities. System/360's true innovation was upgradeability without software or hardware overhaul. Crafted by Gene Amdahl and Fred Brooks, it set a new standard in computer design. Its principles persist in today's System z servers, maintaining the System/360's groundbreaking legacy.

**The first version of BASIC Programming Language is Released - May 1st**

Developed in 1963 at Dartmouth College by John G. Kemeny and Thomas E. Kurtz, BASIC made computing accessible to non-experts, democratizing program creation. Their

John G. Kemeny (left) and Thomas E. Kurtz (right)

Dartmouth Time Sharing System also allowed multiple users to run programs remotely, influencing minicomputer development. BASIC became ubiquitous with the 1970s microcomputer boom, and although its use declined towards the 20th century's end, Microsoft's Visual Basic revitalized its presence in the 1990s. BASIC's introduction and evolution significantly impacted personal computing and programming education, marking it as a cornerstone in the history of computer science.

**Syncom 3: Pioneering Geostationary Satellite Launches - August 19th**

Syncom 3

Syncom 3, the first geostationary satellite, marked a turning point in global communication. Stationed above the equator, it notably broadcast the Tokyo Olympics live, achieving an unprecedented feat of real-time intercontinental connectivity. It also conducted crucial communications tests and served the Department of Defense during the Vietnam War. Positioned at 180 degrees longitude from September 23rd, it synchronized perfectly with Earth's rotation, enhancing teletype and long-distance communications. Retired in April 1969, Syncom 3's legacy in shaping the communication landscape remains unparalleled.

## Moog Synthesizer Revolutionizes Music Production - October 12th

The Moog synthesizer, created by Robert Moog in 1964, revolutionized music with its analog synthesis, offering musicians innovative sound-shaping tools through modules like oscillators and envelope

The Moog Modular Synthesizer

generators. Its introduction of modularity and voltage control paved the way for future synthesizers. Gaining prominence with Wendy Carlos's "Switched-On Bach," the Moog captivated rock icons and stirred debate by mimicking traditional instruments. Its significant influence led to the 1970s' Minimoog, sealing the Moog's indelible impact on music.

## Countdown to Mars: Mariner 4 Begins Epic Journey - November 28th

Mariner 4, part of NASA's quest to explore planets, dramatically changed our view of Mars with its 1964 flyby. It sent the first close-up images of Mars' surface, showing a moon-like, cratered landscape, challenging theories of Martian life. Mariner 4 also studied the interplanetary environment and tested long-haul spaceflight technology. Expected to operate for just eight months, it exceeded its lifespan, continuing for nearly three years. Notably, the mission team created the first digital image by hand with pastels when faced with tape recorder issues, a rendition that closely resembled the actual photos sent by the spacecraft.

Mariner 4

## Fashion

The year 1964 was an electrifying moment in the tapestry of fashion, building upon the kaleidoscope of styles that emerged in 1963. It was a year punctuated by the world's growing appetite for both comfort and rebellious self-expression.

1960s Fashion

Paisley

The 'Beehive' hairdo: Barbra Streisand in 1964

Skirts still danced around the knee, while the audacity of leather and fur was ever-present. However, 1964 saw an even bolder embrace of patterns: paisley became the poster child of bohemian flair, and ascot scarves signified a suave, sophisticated demeanor. The trend of comfort combined with an undeniable style found its epitome in the relaxed waistlines and the ever-versatile shift dress, bidding adieu to the constraining petticoats of the past.

Yet, it was the world of beauty that captured the essence of '64. While the subdued makeup palette of 1963 continued, the 'beehive' hairdo reached new, gravity-defying peaks. Additionally, the daring act of 'ironing' one's hair to achieve poker-straight locks became more commonplace, symbolizing the lengths (or rather, straightness) women would go to for fashion.

For men, the rock 'n' roll wave, led by the indomitable Beatles, continued to shape sartorial choices. Their iconic mop-top was more than just a hairstyle; it was a statement of nonconformity. Meanwhile, trousers streamlined their appearance by shedding front pleats, and striped jackets and sweaters became

Beatles: Mop-top Phase

1960s Men's Fashion

ubiquitous. The color revolution in men's fashion was unstoppable. The once-staid palette exploded into a riot of hues, with fiery reds and sun-kissed yellows taking center stage.

1964 also heralded the rise of androgyny in fashion. Men's and women's styles began to overlap in interesting ways. Turtlenecks paired with vests became a unisex trend, and the blur between masculinity and femininity was further exemplified by women donning trousers and bell bottoms with aplomb. However, the echo of the 1950s was still palpable; gloves, although less frequent, graced the hands of women on special occasions.

Plaid Pants or Sportcoat with Solid Trousers

Mick Jagger wearing a turtleneck sweater while rehearsing

Yet, amidst all this change, the elegance and class of Jackie Kennedy remained a steady beacon. Her influence was unmistakable, with women everywhere emulating her impeccable two-piece suits and iconic pillbox hats.

In essence, 1964 was a year of duality – a bridge between the past and the future. It was a year that celebrated individuality while nodding to tradition, capturing the spirit of an era that was ever-changing, ever evolving. Fashion in 1964 wasn't just about clothes; it was a reflection of the zeitgeist of a generation hungry for change.

Jackie Kennedy's signature outfits

## Cars

In 1964, the automotive world was at a crossroads. The U.S. car industry, amidst the echoes of the Big Three's (General Motors, Ford, and Chrysler) dominance, faced the onset of foreign competition. Mustang's introduction by Ford created a new 'pony car' segment, electrifying consumers. The landscape saw an evolution, as Japanese automakers like Toyota and Honda began their quiet ascent. Still, while the giants solidified their hold, smaller manufacturers grappled with a fast-evolving market. The spirit of '64 epitomized an industry in flux, setting the stage for an automotive revolution.

### Top Selling Cars

### U.S.A

1964 Plymouth Barracuda

Ford's Mustang became an overnight sensation in 1964, marking a new era in automotive design and consumer aspiration. With sales crossing 400,000 units in its first year, its long hood, short deck style, and affordable price tag made it an instant classic. The Mustang's range of customization options and engines, from economical six-cylinders to powerful V8s, offered something for everyone.

Chrysler's Plymouth Barracuda, launched just days before the Mustang, also made waves. With its unique wraparound back glass and sporty design, the Barracuda appealed to a younger generation of drivers. A variety of engine options and trim levels gave it a competitive edge, leading to strong initial sales.

## U.K.

964 Mini Cooper

The Mini Cooper, introduced by the British Motor Corporation (BMC), became a symbol of 1960s British popular culture. Sales were robust, and its compact design combined with nimble handling made it a favorite on British roads. The Mini's iconic status was further cemented by its multiple Monte Carlo Rally wins.

On the luxury front, the Rolls-Royce Silver Cloud III was the car among the elite. With handcrafted interiors, a commanding presence, and a silky-smooth V8 engine, it exemplified British luxury and engineering finesse.

1964 Rolls-Royce Silver Cloud III

1964 Ferrari 250 GTO

### Fastest Car

1964 was a standout year in high-speed automotive excellence. The Ferrari 250 GTO, a marvel in Italian engineering, was in its prime. Designed both for road use and racing, it housed a V12 engine that allowed it to reach

0-60 mph (0-97 km/h) in just over 6 seconds, with a top speed of 174 mph (280 km/h). Its aerodynamic design, combined with its sheer power, made it dominate competitive racing and became an icon in automotive circles.

Competing in prestige and performance, the Shelby Cobra 289 emerged as a symbol of American and British collaboration. With its lightweight design and a powerful Ford V8 engine, it could reach

1964 Shelby Cobra 289

0-60 mph in around 4.9 seconds. Its blend of speed, power, and beauty made it a favorite among enthusiasts.

## Most Expensive American Car of 1964

1964 Cadillac Fleetwood Sixty Special Sedan

The Cadillac Fleetwood Sixty Special stood tall as the epitome of luxury and opulence in 1964. Priced at a hefty $6,652, it was the pinnacle of American luxury. Its elegant design, paired with advanced features like an automatic climate control system, made it an object of desire among the elite. The Fleetwood's plush interiors, including real walnut accents and premium fabrics, made every journey an experience in luxury.

## Most Powerful Muscle Car of 1964

1964 Pontiac GTO

The Pontiac GTO, often credited as the originator of the muscle car genre, was the talk of the town in 1964. Under the hood, it boasted a 389 cubic inch V8 engine, producing 325 horsepower. Optional "Tri-Power" carburetion upped that to 348 horsepower. Its aggressive styling, combined with its raw power and performance, resonated with the youth, and the GTO became an instant legend. This model marked the beginning of a new era in American automotive history, setting the stage for the muscle car battles of the late 60s and early 70s.

## Popular Recreation

Beatlemania: fans scream and shout during a performance

The 1960s were a whirlwind, with each year churning out its own unique blend of culture, controversy, and charm. But if there was one year that managed to distill the decade's essence into twelve short months, it was 1964. A year marked by soaring melodies, momentous achievements, and iconic memories, 1964

1964 "Remco" Beatles Dolls Complete Set

was a jubilant testament to human spirit and creativity. As music pulsed through vinyl records, a British invasion was underway. The Beatles stormed the shores of America, making their debut on "The Ed Sullivan Show." Beatlemania took root, and soon, Fab Four dolls flew off the shelves, becoming coveted collectibles for avid fans. With songs like "I Want to Hold Your Hand" and "Can't Buy Me Love," The Beatles changed the musical landscape forever. The charismatic band was not just producing music; they were symbols of a new, liberated generation, their harmonies echoing the aspirations and dreams of the youth.

Johnny Seven O.M.A.

G.I. Joe: America's Movable Fighting Man

The toy industry was booming with innovations. The Johnny Seven O.M.A. (One Man Army) stormed the market. This multifunction toy weapon, with its seven unique features, became the best-selling boys' toy of 1964, capturing imaginations and topping wish lists. On the other hand, G.I. Joe, with his "21 movable parts," was a sensation, and in only two years, it accounted for over half of Hasbro's sales. No longer referred to as a doll, G.I. Joe was firmly established as an action figure. If that wasn't enough, 1964 saw Mr. Potato Head undergo a significant transformation. Once a toy requiring a real potato, Mr. Potato Head went plastic, adopting a precision-molded, man-made spud body.

1960's Mr. Potato Head

In the realm of games, "Hands Down" became the most popular board game of the year. Crafted by Marvin Glass and Harvey "Hank" Kramer for

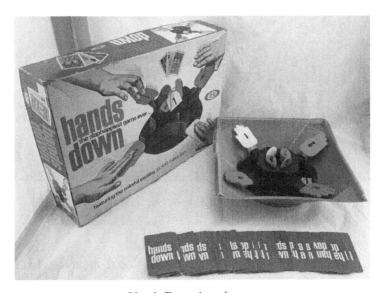

Hands Down board game

Ideal Toy Company, this slap-happy game of pairs and reactions became an instant classic, offering a delightful mix of strategy and speed. Players eagerly slapped down hand-shaped paddles, racing to get their hands in before their competitors.

Television was becoming an indispensable fixture in homes, transforming the way people consumed entertainment. With shows capturing imaginations, including children's programming that marketed Johnny Seven O.M.A., families gathered around the TV for shared experiences. Meanwhile, the iconic James Bond returned to the silver screen with "Goldfinger," ensuring packed theaters and memorable movie nights.

Japan's athlete delegation enters Tokyo's National Stadium during the opening ceremony of the 1964 Summer Olympics

The Tokyo Summer Olympics of 1964 were a global spectacle, bridging countries and cultures in a shared celebration of athleticism and unity, made even more special with advancements like the photo-finish camera and satellite broadcasting.

Bob Dylan's profound lyrics in "The Times They Are a-Changin'" served as a soulful backdrop to a society in flux. Civil rights, freedom, and equality were not just topics of discussion but passionate causes that resonated deeply, both in public forums and private reflections.

Reflecting on 1964, it stands out as a radiant mix of entertainment, activism, and innovation. It was a year where the world sang, played, and progressed, marking indelible memories that still resonate in hearts and histories.

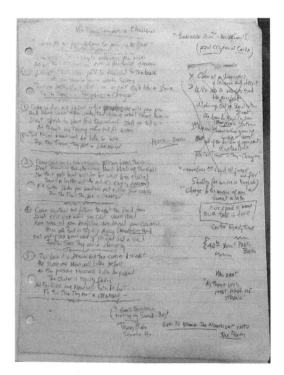

The handwritten lyrics of "The Times They Are a-Changin'"

# **Chapter VI:** Births & Deaths 1964

## **Births (onthisday.com)**

January 7th – Nicolas Cage: American Actor

January 12th – Jeff Bezos: American Entrepreneur

January 17th – Michelle Obama: Former US First Lady

February 11th – Ken Shamrock: American Martial Artist

February 15th – Chris Farley: American Comedian and Actor

February 21st – Scott Kelly: American Astronaut

March 7th – Bret Easton Ellis: American Author

March 7th – Wanda Sykes: American Comedian and Actress

March 10th – Prince Edward: British Royalty

March 29th – Elle MacPherson: Australian Supermodel and Actress

March 30th – Tracy Chapman: American Singer-Songwriter

April 7th – Russell Crowe: Australian-New Zealand Actor

April 24th – Cedric the Entertainer: American Comedian and Actor

April 25th – Hank Azaria: American Actor and Voice Artist

May 13th – Stephen Colbert: American Comedian and TV Host

May 13th – Ronnie Coleman: American Bodybuilder

May 26th – Lenny Kravitz: American Musician

May 30th – Tom Morello: American Guitarist

June 15th – Courtney Cox: American Actress

June 19th – Boris Johnson: British Politician

June 22nd – Dan Brown: American Author

July 9th – Courtney Love: American Musician and Actress

July 22nd – John Leguizamo: Colombian-American Actor

July 22nd – David Spade: American Comedian and Actor

July 24th – Barry Bonds: American Baseball Player

July 26th – Sandra Bullock: American Actress

August 9th – Brett Hull: Canadian-American NHL Player

August 15th – Melinda Gates: American Philanthropist

September 2nd – Keanu Reeves: Canadian Actor

September 10th – Jack Ma: Chinese Entrepreneur

October 3rd – Clive Owen: English Actor

October 9th – Guillermo del Toro: Mexican Film Director

October 20th – Kamala Harris: American Politician and Vice President

December 4th – Marisa Tomei: American Actress

December 18th – Steve Austin. American Pro Wrestler

December 23rd – Eddie Vedder: American Rock Singer

## Deaths (onthisday.com)

January 17th – T. H. White: English Novelist and Author

January 29th – Alan Ladd: American Actor

February 6th – Emilio Aguinaldo: 1st President of the Philippines

March 18th – Norbert Wiener: American Mathematician, Founder of Cybernetics

March 20th – Brendan Behan: Irish Author and Poet

March 23rd – Peter Lorre: Actor Known for Roles in Crime and Mystery Films

April 5th – Douglas MacArthur: American WWII General

April 14th – Rachel Carson: American Marine Biologist and Conservationist

April 23rd – Karl Polanyi: Economic Anthropologist

May 2nd – Nancy Astor: American-Born British Politician

May 27th – Jawaharlal Nehru: 1st Prime Minister of India

May 30th – Leó Szilárd: Nuclear Physicist and Peace Activist

June 9th – Max Aitken, 1st Baron Beaverbrook: British Newspaper Publisher and Politician

June 11th – Plaek Phibunsongkhram: Thai Military Officer and Politician

August 3rd – Flannery O'Connor: American Novelist and Short Story Writer

August 21st – Palmiro Togliatti: Italian Politician

September 18th – Seán O'Casey: Irish Dramatist and Memoirist

October 10th – Eddie Cantor: American "Banjo Eyes" Comedian, Singer, Actor, and Songwriter

October 15th – Cole Porter: American Composer and Lyricist

October 20th – Herbert Hoover: 31st President of the United States

November 16th – Piet Moeskops: Dutch Track Cyclist

December 1st – J. B. S. Haldane: British-Indian Scientist and Geneticist

# Chapter VII: Statistics 1964

* U.S. GDP 1964 – 685,8 billion USD (worldbank.org)

* U.S. GDP 2022 – 25.46 trillion USD (worldbank.org)

* U.K. GDP 1964 – 94.1 billion USD (worldbank.org)

* U.K. GDP 2022 – 3.07 trillion USD (worldbank.org)

* U.S. Inflation 1964 – 1.31% (officialdata.org)

* U.S. Inflation 2022 – 8.0% (worldbank.org)

* U.K. Inflation 1964 – 3.33% (officialdata.org)

* U.K. Inflation 2022 – 7.9% (worldbank.org)

* U.S. Population 1964 – 190,895,000 (census.gov)

* U.S. Population 2022 - 333,287,557 (worldbank.org)

* U.K. Population 1964 – 53,861,500 (macrotrends.net)

* U.K. Population 2022 - 66,971.41 (worldbank.org)

* U.S. Life Expectancy at Birth 1964 - 70.17 (countryeconomy.com)

* U.S. Life Expectancy at Birth 2022 - 79.05 (www.macrotrends.net)

* U.K. Life Expectancy at Birth 1964 – 71.62 (countryeconomy.com)

* U.K. Life Expectancy at Birth 2022 – 81.65 (www.macrotrends.net)

* U.S. Annual Working Hours Per Worker 1964 - 1,933 (ourworldindata.org)

* U.S. Annual Working Hours Per Worker 2017 - 1,757 (ourworldindata.org)

* U.K. Annual Working Hours Per Worker 1964 - 2,021 (ourworldindata.org)

* U.K. Annual Working Hours Per Worker 2017 - 1,670 (ourworldindata.org)

* U.S. Unemployment Rate 1964 – 5.0% (thebalancemoney.com)

* U.S. Unemployment Rate 2022 – 3.6% (worldbank.org)

* U.K. Unemployment Rate 1964 - 1.6% (fullfact.org)

* U.K. Unemployment Rate 2022 – 3.7% (ons.gov.uk)

* U.S. Tax Revenue (% of GDP) 1964 – 16.5% (fred.stlouisfed.org)

* U.S. Tax Revenue (% of GDP) 2021 – 11.2% (worldbank.org)

* U.K. Tax Revenue (% of GDP) 1964 – 32.5% (ukpublicrevenue.co.uk)

* U.K. Tax Revenue (% of GDP) 2021 – 26.4% (worldbank.org)

* U.S. Prison Population 1964 - 214,336 (bjs.ojp.gov)

* U.S. Prison Population 2021 - 1,204,300 (bjs.ojp.gov)

* U.K. Prison Population 1964 - 33,809 (parliament.uk)

* U.K. Prison Population 2022 - 81,806 (gov.uk)

* U.S. Average Cost of a New House 1964 – $18,900 (gobankingrates.com)

* U.S. Average Cost of a New House 2022 – $454,900 (gobankingrates.com)

* U.K. Average Cost of a New House 1964 – £3,104 (loveproperty.com)

* U.K. Average Cost of a New House 2022 – £296,000 (ons.gov.uk)

* U.S. Average Income per Year 1964 – $6,600 (census.gov)

* U.S. Average Income per Year US 2022 – $56,368 (demandsage.com)

* U.K. Average Income per Year 1964 – £1,997 (theguardian.com)

* U.K. Average Income per Year 2022 – £33,000 (gov.uk)

* U.S. Cost of Living: The $100 from 1964 has grown to about $992.87 today, up $892.87 over 59 years due to an average yearly inflation of 3.97%, resulting in a 892.87% total price hike (in2013dollars.com).

* U.K. Cost of Living: Today's £2,499.06 mirrors the purchasing power of £100 in 1964, showing a £2,399.06 hike over 59 years. The pound's yearly inflation rate averaged 5.61% during this period, leading to a 2,399.06% total price rise (in2013dollars.com).

## Cost Of Things

### United States

* Men's coat, lightweight cardigan: $15.95 (mclib.info)

* Women's coat, seersucker suit: $11.98 (mclib.info)

* Women's handbag: $1.99-$3.00 (mclib.info)

* Fresh eggs (1 dozen): $0.54 (stacker.com)

* White bread (1 pound): $0.21 (stacker.com)

* Sliced bacon (1 pound): $0.67 (stacker.com)

* Round steak (1 pound): $1.04 (stacker.com)

* Potatoes (10 pounds): $0.76 (stacker.com)

* Fresh delivered milk (1/2 gallon): $0.53 (stacker.com)

* Price per gallon (petrol): $0.29 (mclib.info)

* Automobiles (Fords): $1,764.00 (mclib.info)

* Bananas: $0.15/lb (mclib.info)

* Cereal, Kellogg's Corn Flakes: $1.00/3 8oz pkgs (mclib.info)

* Margarine, Fleischmann's: $0.42/lb (mclib.info)

* Mayonnaise, Hellmann's: $0.59/quart (mclib.info)

* Onions, Texas: $0.25/3 lbs (mclib.info)

* Oranges, Florida: $0.49/4lb bag (mclib.info)

* Peanut butter: $0.99/3lb jar (mclib.info)

* Potatoes, Maine: $0.45/5lbs (mclib.info)

**United Kingdom (retrowow.co.uk)**

* Gallon of petrol: 5s 1d

* Pint of beer: 2s 3d

* Bulmer's Dry Cider 38 fl. oz.: 2s 9d

* 20 cigarettes: 4s 11d

* Pint of milk: 9d

* 19" KB Westminster black & white TV (Currys): 59½ guineas

* The Daily Mirror newspaper: 3d to 4d

* Pepsi Cola can (Vivo): 10½d

* Elite refrigerator: £37 16s

* Hoover Keymatic 3224 - automatic washing machine: £99 15s

* Qualcast Punch Mk VII petrol lawnmower: £29 19s 6d

* Wall's pork sausages 1lb: 3s 4d

* Macleans Value toothpaste - tube: 3s 2d

* ½lb margarine (Vivo): 7½d

* Moulton Standard M1 small wheel bicycle: £26 9s 6d

* 1 cwt of coal delivered: 8s to 12s

* Ekco Princess electric blanket: £10 0s 2d

# **Chapter VIII:** Iconic Advertisements of 1964

Martini Bianco

Chevrolet Chevy II Nova

IBM Selectric Typewriter

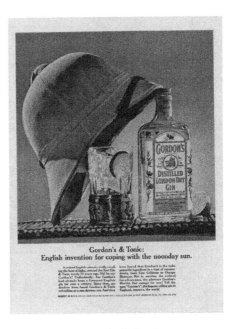

Gordon's Gin

Firestone

Pan Am

Campbell's Soup

Jim Beam

## SONY Now Offers a Choice In Personal Television

Regardless of the model you select, you choose the finest when you buy SONY personal, truly portable television. Whether it's the remarkable 8-lb. Micro-TV with 5" screen or the new 12-lb. Model 9-304W with 9" screen, it operates on its own rechargeable battery pack, auto/boat power and AC. Designed by SONY, developer of the transistorized pocketable radio and leader in the field of transistor electronics, the 27-transistor Model 9-304W introduces innovations which make it

unique. Included are a new rectangular picture tube with sensitivity and resolution superior to ordinary sets to special accessory filter provides unsurpassed resolution even in bright daylight); new Mesa transistors for increased sensitivity; automatic gain control for better picture stability; 1/10th the power consumption of ordinary sets and practically no heat. A full series of accessories, including battery pack and UHF adaptor, is available for both models.

**SONY**
RESEARCH MAKES THE DIFFERENCE

SONY CORPORATION OF AMERICA • 580 FIFTH AVE., 74Y, 36, N.Y. • REGIONAL OFFICES, LOS ANGELES • CHICAGO
CAR and DRIVER

Sony Personal Television

Actual photograph of water running out of other catsup, 3 minutes 39 seconds after both were poured.

One reason you may pay a little more for Heinz.

Heinz Tomato Ketchup

**now it's Pepsi-for those who think young**

Thinking young is in the wind from coast to coast. We're on the lookout for fun—the right outlook for Pepsi! Its sparkling-light taste is so inviting, so clean, so welcome. And ice-cold Pepsi-Cola drenches your thirst, refreshes like no other. So think young . . . say "Pepsi, please!"

**PEPSI-COLA**

Pepsi-Cola

Lucky Strike

Dickies Jeans

Smirnoff Vodka

Volkswagen

Kodak Cameras                    Kellogg's Corn Flakes

7 Up                    Marlboro

Colgate

Jose Cuervo Tequilla

64' Pontiac

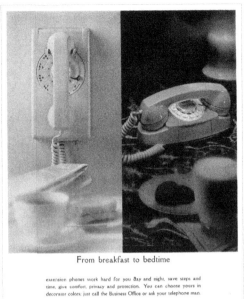

From breakfast to bedtime

extension phones work hard for you day and night, save steps and time, give comfort, privacy and protection. You can choose yours in decorator colors; just call the Business Office or ask your telephone man.

BELL TELEPHONE SYSTEM
Serving you

Bell Telephone System

Did you know that substantial, body-building Quaker Oats also fits into an adult weight-control program?

Cooks in just one minute...
costs less than 2 cents a serving!

Quaker Oats

Things go better with Coke

Coca-Cola

Do you keep reaching for taste that's not really there?

Camel's real taste satisfies longer!

The best tobacco makes the best smoke!

Get with Camel—a real cigarette!

Camel

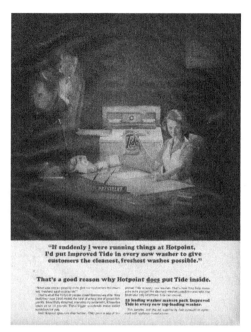

Tide

Budweiser

64' Chrysler Dodge

# I have a gift for you!

Dear reader, thank you so much for reading my book!

To make this book more (much more!) affordable, all images are in black and white, but I've created a special gift for you!

You can now have access, for FREE, to the PDF version of this book with the original images!

Keep in mind that some are originally black and white, but some are colored.

I hope you enjoy it!

Please leave a positive book review here:

bit.ly/3GsQ7FD

*Or* Scan this QR Code:

# I have a favor to ask you!

I deeply hope you've enjoyed reading this book and felt transported right into 1964!

I loved researching it, organizing it, and writing it, knowing that it would make your day a little brighter.

If you've enjoyed it too, I would be extremely grateful if you took just a few minutes to leave a positive customer review and share it with your friends.

As an unknown author, that makes all the difference and gives me the extra energy I need to keep researching, writing, and bringing joy to all my readers. Thank you!

*Best regards,*
*Robert E. Taylor*

Please leave a positive book review here:

amzn.to/3GuG2rP

*Or* Scan this QR Code:

# Discover All the Books in This Collection!

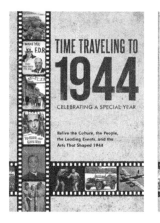

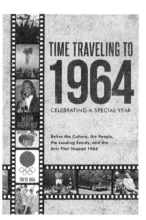

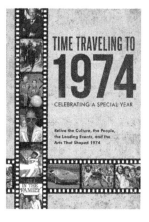

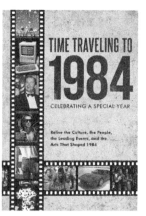

Made in the USA
Las Vegas, NV
04 December 2024

13355650R00059